The Pampered Prince

The Pampered Prince

TIPS AND TECHNIQUES ON BUILDING
A GREAT RELATIONSHIP WITH YOUR SON

C. Lynn Williams

The Pampered Prince
by C. Lynn Williams

Cover Design by Atinad Designs.

© Copyright 2012

SAINT PAUL PRESS, DALLAS, TEXAS

First Printing, 2012

The name SAINT PAUL PRESS and its logo are registered as a trademark in the U.S. patent office.

ISBN-10: 0-9854258-5-7
ISBN-13: 978-0-9854258-5-2

Printed in the U.S.A.

Praise for *The Pampered Prince*

"A great solution to bring mothers and their sons together. Enjoy this book!"
MICHAEL RAY DRESSER,
TALK SHOW HOST AND MEDIA COACH
DRESSER AFTER DARK

"C. Lynn Williams does a wonderful job of discussing the intricacies of mother and son relationships. This is a must for every mother. Dads and sons – don't wait for Mother's Day, this is the next book you buy for mom!"
ANN McINDOO, SPEAKER AND AUTHOR OF *SO YOU WANT TO WRITE!* AND *7 EASY STEPS TO WRITE YOUR BOOK*

"Many young boys have different experiences with their mothers: some dependent, some estranged, and most healthy. C. Lynn Williams offers a great perspective that helps mothers create strong positive relationships with their sons. Great book!"
CANDACE WILLIAMS, MSW, LCSW CLINICAL CASE MANAGER

Also by *C. Lynn Williams*

Trying to Stay Sane While Raising Your Teen:
A Primer for Parents

Your children are not your children.
They are sons and daughters of Life's longing for itself.
They come through you but not from you.
And though they are with you yet they belong not to you.
You may give them your love but not your thoughts,
for they have their own thoughts.
You may house their bodies but not their souls,
for their souls dwell in the house of tomorrow,
which you cannot visit, not even in your dreams.
You may strive to be like them,
but seek not to make them like you.

THE PROPHET, KHALIL GIBRAN

All grown-ups were children first.
(But few remember it.)

THE LITTLE PRINCE,
ANTOINE DE SAINT-EXUPERY

Acknowledgements

I would like to thank my wonderful children, Candace, Alex, Jackie and Jay. You are always in my heart. Thank you to my family and friends who responded every time I needed feedback, insight, and proofreaders. A special thank you to my sister and friends, Iris Cochran, Carolyn Stewart, Velvet Hawkins and Holly DuPart, for being available to read or answer every question that I presented to them.

Thank you to my author coach, Ann McIndoo, who helped me manage deadlines. Thank you to my publisher, St. Paul Press, as well as others, who opened the world of marketing and promotions to me.

Finally, thank you to my husband, Jimmy. May you always be the wind beneath my wings.

C. Lynn Williams

Contents

Foreword

by Reverend Dr. Jeremiah A. Wright, Jr.
Pastor Emeritus, Trinity United Church of Christ

C. Lynn Williams has written an exceptionally helpful book for mothers who are trying to raise their sons in the rapidly changing culture of the 21st century. Fathers of boys will also be helped by C. Lynn Williams' book, but her book is written specifically for and addressed to mothers who are engaged in this awesome task. I read her book with great interest and forty-four years of experience as an ordained minister. In my pastoral work (both as an Assistant Pastor and as a Senior Pastor), I have spent countless hours counseling young boys, talking to parents of young boys and working with mothers who were trying to negotiate the rocky terrain of raising their sons from boyhood to manhood.

I came to C. Lynn Williams' text with a strong academic background in the field she has chosen for this, her second book. I had read her first book, *Trying to Stay Sane While Raising Your Teen*, and I was anxious to see what she could add to that exciting and helpful guidebook.

The academic background that I brought to the

reading of this text started with Dr. Na'im Akbar's, *Visions for Black Men* (1991). Dr. Akbar was one of the founding members of the Association of Black Psychologists. Dr. Akbar wrote about the three stages that all males go through on this journey from boyhood to manhood - - the male stage, the boy stage and the man stage. Dr. Akbar's insights are invaluable. Ms. Williams echoes some of what Akbar's findings show. Dr. Akbar did not write and he does not speak, however, as a Black mother who has raised two African-American boys in the 20th and 21st centuries!

One of the former members of our church, Dr. Jawanzaa Kunjufu published a four-volume guidebook back in the 1990's (1995) and his work, *Countering the Conspiracy to Destroy Black Boys*, offers some important tips about the educational process both within and beyond the boundaries of the academic school systems of America. Dr. Kunjufu, however, does not write as a Black woman who has nurtured Black boys both in her classrooms and in her home!

In 1993, one of my colleagues in ministry, the Reverend Dr. T. Garrott Benjamin, (Pastor of the Light of the World Christian Church in Indianapolis) wrote a book about this same topic. His book, *Boys to Men: A Handbook for Survival*, is written from the vantage point of a Pastor who is serving and has served an urban Black congregation for over four decades.

Dr. Benjamin offers insights that help parents to understand the dynamics involved in a gang culture, a drug culture, a culture of "nihilism," to use Dr. Cornel

West's term. Rev. T. Garrott Benjamin, however, does not write as a mother. He is a parent. He has done an awesome job in raising his children as a Black father living in the home with his "Manchild in the Promised Land." He cannot offer the insights, however, that Ms. Williams offers in her work because he is not a Black mother!

My classmate at Virginia Union University, Dr. Anderson J. Franklin has written an important guidebook for parents who are seeking to raise Black boys in the 21st century. Published in 2004, Dr. Franklin's book, *From Brotherhood to Manhood: How Black Men Rescue Their Relationships and Dreams from the Invisibility Syndrome*, gives a psychologist's point of view and perspective for parents who have to teach their young African-American off-spring core values in a society that is saturated and is also suffocating from racism! Dr. Franklin is also a Founding Member of the Association of Black Psychologists. He is not a Black mother, however!

C. Lynn writes from the vantage point of a Black woman. C. Lynn writes as a Black mother who has successfully created healthy relationships with her sons and she offers her insights, her advice and her observations from the vantage point of a mother who has "walked the walk."

Ms. Williams offers helpful guidelines for avoiding the pitfalls of modernity while establishing core values, spiritual values and a healthy context of love and support for all mothers who take seriously the important task that God has given them in giving them a "manchild" to raise in today's world.

I am sure you will be blessed by the insights she offers.

Preface

Spirit tells me that children are a gift from the Lord, a reward from him. I truly believe that, and I know that what you put into your relationship with your children, you receive it back in amazing ways. Have you ever bought your child a gift to show them that you love them? Buying your kids everything they want or giving them everything on their wish list is definitely not what I am telling you to do, but what I am suggesting is that you give them a more intangible gift: your time. Tell them about your experiences growing up (the ones you are proud of as well as those that you would like to forget). Do things with your kids that they enjoy. Can you rollerblade or skateboard? How about going bowling or playing a game of basketball or jump rope? Attend their events, and be present with your children. Being present does not mean that while you are with them you can talk on your cell phone or continuously text other people. You might as well be absent. Kids know when you are spending time with them or just giving them lip service.

Also, don't be surprised if your child acts disinterested and tells you how 'ole skool' you are when you tell them you want to spend time with them. We used to tell my mother, 'No other kids have to have cultural night. Why do we?' Cultural night was a night during the week that my mother would play songs on the piano and we would all sing together. Most of the songs we did not know because we had never heard them before. However, it wasn't long before we looked forward to cultural night. It was corny, but it gave us time together as a family. A lot of whether something is right or wrong is based on whether your child's peers approve of it or not. That peer pressure is especially important if you are not giving your child family traditions and experiences that are both fun and will teach them right from wrong. In the long run, build a lifelong foundation of love and support that your child will have to draw upon and remember forever. I believe external factors like gangs and pimps are able to prey on our children more if we are NOT giving them the love and attention at home that they are starving for.

Today there are so many distractions and complexities to "growing up". Technology alone has accelerated the pace in which we are living our lives. The social networks and the ability to communicate with anyone who has access to the Internet, means our children don't stay young and innocent very long. So while your child is young and impressionable, take time to create memorable experiences. Develop a lifelong relationship with your son or daughter. Become your son's hero. Meditate on and with him or her, so that they are aware of a higher powerful divinity; and are spiritual warriors for their own friends.

Most of all, operate with integrity because it is not what you say that impacts your child, it's what you do and your behaviors that they model. You can't tell your son not to smoke marijuana, and then come home high. Children see that. Model the behavior you want to see in them. Will you make mistakes? Yes, of course you will; we all make mistakes. It's what you do after you've made the mistake that matters. Operate with honor and integrity!

Introduction

As I was finishing my first book, *Trying to Stay Sane While Raising Your Teen*, available on Amazon.com, I started feeling that the rest of the story had not been told. I meditated about it for a couple of weeks, and realized that I had a message for mothers who had birthed, raised, worried about, or cared for sons. I know that I wasn't the only one who wanted a wonderful relationship with my sons. Mothers everywhere want the same thing too, and while I don't profess to know everything there is to know about parenting boys into men, I have a lot of experience to share with you.

If you are a single mother, teen mother, stepmother, grandmother, adoptive mother, kinship caregiver, foster mother, legal guardian or woman who has mothered boys without ever having had the title of mom, there is hope for you. As mothers, we are used to giving everything we have to our children and when the relationship is strong and wonderful, there is nothing like it, life is great! However, when we don't see eye to eye or, our sons get into trouble constantly or, they don't listen to our advice or they simply ignore us, it hurts our hearts. I know mine does. The title, "The Pampered Prince" is in honor of our sons who are like princes to us. We pamper them, love them and worry about them and while they make our hearts proud, sometimes they act like spoiled brats. We love them in spite of their faults, and this book offers stories and practical tips to help you build a more rewarding and wonderful relationship with your son.

Chapter One
My Son, My Heart

I wonder what happens when mothers realize that their baby being born is a boy. Does it differ a lot from having a girl? How is a boy celebrated? I know that men pass out cigars, and sometimes name their sons after their fathers. But what happens to mothers after their sons are born? When my son was born, he was a lot different than his sister. For one thing, he was calmer and didn't cry a lot. Girls come into the world with a lot to say, and start telling you how they feel as soon as they are born!

My son seemed content with his surroundings and watched everything that went on around him. I don't know if I fell in love with his calmness or maybe I was more experienced as a mother, so our experience together was more enjoyable. The other thing that made our life together very special was that I had had a miscarriage before he was born and had started experiencing the same symptoms when carrying him. However, those symptoms stopped early in my pregnancy and we were blessed with a big bundle of joy.

For some women, their son becomes their "little man". This can occur whether she has a husband, a significant other or no one. You might say, well, what's wrong with the phrase "little man"? Nothing is wrong if it were just a phrase. But we all know a phrase is never "just a phrase". Phrases have meanings whether conscious or unconscious. The phrase connotes more of an unnatural relationship, one that is more a boyfriend and girlfriend type, instead of a mother and son. A son will never be a woman's boyfriend. And I am sure that if a mother thought of how the phrase sounds to people outside of her circle of friends and family, she wouldn't use it.

I remember Anna from Ohio had two children, a boy and a girl. Her son was born five years after his sister, and the family was delighted that their second child was a boy. They had been trying for a second child, had had some difficulties and once he was born, he quickly became the mom's favorite child. She called him her "little man". He could do no wrong. Of course you can imagine what problems it created for the entire family: the husband resented his wife's relationship; the daughter loved her brother, but was starved for attention from her mother; and the boy needed a more realistic relationship with his mother, one that taught him consequences and held him accountable.

A man becomes a man after having lived through many life experiences as a boy. There are stages he goes through: baby, toddler, young boy, adolescent, teen (young and older) and then manhood. In order for your son to become a man he has to successfully live through each of those periods in his life. Sometimes those periods become interrupted as a result of how the boy's life matriculates. Maybe he loses his dad, and has to help out with the bills; so he works and goes to school. That's a very maturing life experience for a young boy to go through. Another life experience that prematurely matures our young men is to become a teen father. Often when parents realize that their son has gotten a girl pregnant, they tell him that the baby is probably not his, or sometimes they advise him to convince the girl to have an abortion. No matter what your personal views are of teen pregnancies, why not have an honest conversation with your son and ask him how he thinks he and the girl should handle the situation. It is a very serious responsibility. In my parents' day, if a boy got a girl pregnant, he had to marry her. While you may not want your son's life to change by becoming a young parent, your advice will also color his relationship with you forever. Impart honorable traits into his personality every time you can, so that he will grow into the man you always expected him to be.

I believe that we set our sons up for disaster at the very beginning of their young life, when we make them feel that they belong solely to us (as their mothers). Fathers probably do the same thing with their daughters; however that is a topic for another book. Don't get me wrong, your sons and daughters belong to you as far as being part of a family is concerned. However a New

Testament passage says "Children, obey your parents because you belong to the Lord and it is the right thing to do". Our sons and daughters are on loan to us for as long as God has decided they will be with us. As parents we are stewards, responsible for loving, nurturing, guiding, disciplining and preparing them to become self-sufficient adults.

In our society, we are probably doing a decent job of parenting our daughters, or it could be that girls are more self-sufficient and durable. If we aren't doing a good job of raising our daughters, we may not know it until she is in her late teens and starts to rebel. We could do a better job of nurturing and loving them as well as sharing our life experiences with them. However, despite us, our girls grow up, graduate from school, get a job and usually move out of the family domicile. The same is not necessarily true for our sons. One third of males age 22 – 34 still live at home.

While your son is in his early twenties, you may not be concerned with having him live at home. You might say, "Well, at least we know where he is." However, what is he doing while he lives with you? Is he working, going to school, doing both? Or is he sleeping late, hanging out with his friends, coming in at all hours of the night? Do you allow women to spend the night in your son's room with him? What are the house rules? Are there house rules or do you allow him to do what he wants?

Do you still perform the motherly duties for him that you performed when he was a youngster, like cooking dinner, fixing his plate, washing, folding and ironing his clothes? Those duties are acceptable when he is 12 years old; however, it is not okay if he is 23. What have you done to prepare him for living on his own? By the way, why should he move out when he is being taken care of so royally by you? I mean, he's the pampered prince, right?

Study Guide Questions

1. Write down the kind of relationship you have with your son?

2. Does he have chores? If yes, what are the consequences if he doesn't do them?

3. Do you pay your son's bills? Does he pay your bills? Explain if you answered yes to either question.

Chapter Two
Oedipus Complex

According to Sigmund Freud, a psychologist in the early 19th century, the Oedipus complex was a theory he used to describe a boy's psychosexual stages of development where the boy desires to be sexually involved with his mother, and has intense feelings of jealousy and anger against his father.[1] This development occurs between the ages of three and five, and is a particularly important stage for boys because it is a time where our sons realize that there is a difference between their mother and their father[2]. They begin to realize that they are more like their fathers, allowing them to become aware of their gender as males, and they start to unconsciously distance themselves from their mothers. So one minute our son is our little buddy, and before you know it, they no longer sit on your lap and hug you for hours.

Two important points here are: boys realize that we as mothers have affections for others besides our sons, and boys become more independent of us as their mothers. There is a theory that the separation that boys begin to experience (from their mothers) can be played out as scorn, a general sense of mastery over women or the unavailability of women[3].

Whether or not you are familiar with the term, Oedipus complex, you are familiar with the times that your son pushes your husband away if you two are sitting too close to each other, or if he punches your husband for kissing or hugging you. I remember having to be careful when we shut our bedroom door around my son to avoid his knocking at our door and yelling "let my mom out of that room". I also remember when I used to be able to walk down the street hand-in-hand with my son, until one day he no longer wanted to be seen being affectionate with me. These are normal stages of development with our boys and eventually the boundaries will relax again between the two of you, to the extent that you and your son will be able to reestablish close ties with each other without the jealousy that occurred when he was much younger.

What do you do when your son exhibits jealousy into his teen years and doesn't want to 'share' you with anyone else? Think about what has occurred in the last couple of years? Have you been in an unsafe relationship, have recently divorced or had a number of relationships over a short period of time? Our children are very much in sync with our emotions and are affected by them whether we openly display any fears or concerns. Our children will be especially protective of us, and our sons may feel that they have to 'fight' our battles for us. If those are not situations that are occurring in your household, and your son is still exhibiting jealous tendencies toward people who are attracted to you, feel free to consult your child's school psychologist or a family therapist for assistance.

Study Guide Questions

1. How old is your son?

2. How do you currently handle your son's displays of jealousy or exaggerated closeness to you?

3. List some ways in which you can support your son through this stage of emotional development:

---

[1] About.com - Psychology
[2] Changing Minds.org
[3] ibid

Chapter Three
Single Mothers Who Parent

If you think that raising kids is easy, ask any parent currently raising kids to give you a five minute summary about their life (routine) with their kids. You are busy, busy, busy! There's always something to do, some place to be, or money to pay out. However, while single parents have the same responsibility as dual parents, for all practical purposes, they operate alone. You may have your mom, dad, an ex-spouse or significant other to talk to, however you are raising those kids by yourself. Usually if you have to get up at night with your child, it's the same you getting up in the morning, when you have to take that child to day care, school, sitter, and then go to work. I think it's important to mention, that as a single parent you feel totally responsible (and maybe even guilty) for the care and keeping of your child.

You may ask, *what do you mean – guilty. I don't feel guilty!* Maybe you don't feel guilty. I know I did. I felt that I had failed my children and my family. I was divorced; something that I never thought would happen to me or my family. And yet, there I was raising two children alone. It may not be your fault that you are alone raising your child. Maybe your spouse died, you divorced, or there was no spouse. However, if your child's father is alive and a responsible person, meaning he pays child support, and/or just wants to be involved in his kids' lives, then include him. There are many men who are not a part of their child's life, so even if your child's father makes you angry every time you see him, remember your son or daughter is delighted to see him. It's really about your son or daughter, right?

This is a chapter on single mothers who parent, or women raising a son without the benefit of a man living in the household. Mothers, we often raise our daughters and love our sons. It is really an unfair parenting phenomenon, but it happens, and it's so innocuous, that most women don't realize that they are perpetuating this. Here is an example: The house is a mess! There is stuff everywhere. You tell your children that you expect the chores to be completed along with their homework, by the time you get home from work. Your daughter's chore was to start dinner and your son's chore was to take out the garbage. Neither chore is done when you arrive home from work, and each child has an excuse. You put your daughter on punishment (she's older) and you fuss at your son. "Charles, I told you to take the garbage out". End of fussing. Guess what – you did it! You have loved your son and parented your daughter. They are both guilty of breaking the house rules and both should be reprimanded equally. If you don't reprimand them both equally, then the son eventually feels that your word has no consequences, he is not accountable and he starts to take advantage of your lack of parenting (for him).

Often, we don't hold our sons accountable for their actions. As one writer puts it "we shield our sons from responsibility".[4] We give excuses for why they don't follow through on behaving, completing chores, school, or getting a job; the list goes on. As a high school teacher, I have heard the phrase: boys will be boys. It's a ridiculous phrase because it points to our cultural inability to hold boys accountable for the same things that we hold girls accountable for. You may decide that as long as your son grows up, everything will be okay. However, the problem with that theory is that instead of a nation of responsible men who will run companies, head households, and raise families, you have men with no internal sense of direction or accountability.[5]

This phenomenon occurs throughout the world in families of all ethnicities, religions, and races. It doesn't matter if you are Caucasian, African American, Hispanic or Asian; poor or rich, rural, urban or suburban. However, as a result of not holding our sons accountable for their actions, many of them end up in prison, unemployed or dead.

If you recognize yourself within these pages then start now to hold your son accountable and responsible for the things you expect him to do. There have to be consequences when he disobeys or breaks rules whether in the house or at school. Yes, he is a boy, but boys will only continue to be boys when we allow that to happen and don't hold them accountable.

Kate from Kansas is struggling with these issues because her son is 20 years old, has dropped out of college and still lives at home. She keeps hoping if she ignores him, he will get the message and either find a job or go back to school. It doesn't happen that easily! Even though he is 20 years old, he is not a man until he has begun to handle adult responsibilities like paying rent and taking care of himself without your help or the help of his father and other relatives.

Also remember that your son is NOT the man in your life. If he still lives at home and works, it is acceptable to expect him to contribute toward the household. You would expect your daughter to do the same. Janice from Chicago has two adult children living at home. While her daughter will attend college in the fall, her son dropped out of college a couple of years ago and works several jobs. When Janice runs out of money, she expects her son to give it to her. When she needs a back rub, she expects her son to give her one, and if she needs work done on her car, she expects her son to take care of it. Mothers it is not your son's responsibility to be at your beck and call (unless you are ill and he is your caregiver), give you money when you run out, or be your "boo." Let your son grow up and be a successful, honest man of integrity, who is able to respect women because of his great relationship with you, his mother.

What if you are an aunt, grandmother or legal guardian who is raising a young man who is not your biological son? As an aunt or grandmother, you have probably known this boy since birth, so hopefully you have more of a relationship with him than if the court awarded you custody, because you are an available foster mom or legal guardian. How do you build a parent/child relationship when you hardly know this child? Relationships are built on love, support, consistent time together and discipline. Thirty to forty years ago, it was common for people to have children in their twenties. My mother was twenty-one when I was born and she said she liked that because she was young enough to enjoy us, and would be relatively young once my siblings and I grew up.

A friend of mine was single and forty when she had her children. She said she was delighted because she wasn't young and immature; she was financially prepared to raise them. I also know women who have had children when they were teens themselves. It wasn't easy, because teens are still growing and maturing and are often not emotionally ready to make the sacrifices required to give their child everything necessary to grow up healthy and whole. What about grandmothers who have become parents as a result of life issues that occur when their adult children have either died, turned to drugs or alcohol, are military soldiers fighting wars, or who are simply unable to raise their own children. Grandmothers have raised their children and are at the time in their life where they should be able to take it easy; to see their grandchildren occasionally but be able to send them home with their mom and dad. Grandmothers are probably the most at-risk parent because they are older, unprepared for the onslaught of issues facing youth today, often exhausted and less prepared to handle the necessary discipline issues that are required to guide their grandsons, now known as their 'sons'. As a female parent whatever your title and however you got the responsibility, it is definitely possible to develop a wonderful relationship with the young man who calls you "mom". Continue to draw upon your belief system and others around you for support. Be sure to take time each day, maybe 15 minutes, to meditate, collect your thoughts, organize your day and prepare yourself for the wonderful experiences you will have with your son.

[4] atlantapost.com – Charing Ball, June 21, 2011
[5] Boys Project – Judy Kleinfield

Study Guide Questions

1. Do you have chores for your son and your daughter?

2. Do you have expectations for your son that are different for your daughter? If yes, please explain.

3. Are the consequences equal? In other words how do you handle your son versus your daughter if they don't obey you?

4. What does the phrase 'Women love their sons and parent their daughters' mean to you?

5. How do you treat your son?

Chapter Four
You Will Always Be My Little Boy

I still remember the first time I heard my son laugh. He was about three months old and his sister would make funny faces to make him laugh. That laughter was a giggle and it was infectious. When he giggled, I would laugh too. I will always remember it and it is memories like that, that endear our children to us forever. There are lots of memories of good times, when our sons are small children or when special events occur in their lives. However, as our sons mature, these memories of them as our little boys, can keep us from allowing our sons to grow into self-sufficient men. In your eyes, he will always be that five-year-old that brought you dandelions thinking they were a wonderful bouquet of flowers that you would love. And you did, simply because they were a gift from your son. That's a wonderful memory, but it is not helpful when your son is struggling to find his way as an adolescent or teen.

As mothers, we are so used to 'doing' for our sons that we continue to wash his laundry, even if he is twenty-something. Did you notice I did not include daughters? Hmm... As a twenty-something year old, most girls are washing their own laundry, maybe everyone else's in the house as well. That's if she is still living at home. Boys on the other hand, continue to accept our good natured help without any rancor or misgivings. If you offer or are willing to wash his clothes, clean his room, cook special meals for him, he will accept it gladly! What child wouldn't accept that offer? However, don't call him a sloth later because he won't wash his laundry or cook his meals.

Don't get me wrong, if you wash household laundry and your son's is a part of that, continue to do that. However, part of teaching responsibility is requiring that our children (sons and daughters) are able to be self-sufficient. I had friends who would not allow their sons to wash dishes or clothes. I thought it was weird because eventually your children grow up and move out. If you haven't set guidelines, shown him how to perform chores like washing clothes, dishes and floors and cooking, how is he going to live on his own, or support that wonderful woman that he falls in love with?

I remember a woman whose husband and son celebrated the same birthday. It was clear this son was the apple of her eye. For his 30th birthday, the mother planned a surprise birthday party for him. However, she had no special birthday plans for her husband. That plan would have probably worked had both she and her husband planned the party for him, but that wasn't what happened. Her son also had a significant other, who was not included in the planning process. In addition, she did not acknowledge her husband's birthday. Pretty messy! Don't get me wrong, as mothers we know the special things our family likes and we delight in seeing their pleasure when we are able to give them those satisfying experiences. However, it is troublesome when we continue to single out our boys and treat them like kings when everyone else in the family is treated like a peasant. This theory is also true when it comes to working out problems. Personally, I am a problem-solver. I will talk to a perfect stranger about how to solve a problem if they ask me; sometimes if I overhear them talking about a problem, I will offer my advice. Boys are different; they need to work out their own issues in order to mature. It builds self-esteem and a maturity that they can't get when we as mothers (and dads) constantly step in to help.

Allowing my son to work out his problems is one of the hardest parenting lessons that I have had to learn and am still learning. Sometimes the answers that are perfectly clear to us as parents are not clear to our sons or daughters. That has to be okay; our sons have to search out the answers in their timeframe. Listening is a useful skill for us as parents during these times, because if he trusts you, then he will most likely talk with you about a problem that he is facing. I have often misunderstood that when they talk, it means I should be giving advice. No! Keep your opinions and thoughts to yourself until your son asks for it.

Another tip I learned from my husband was that even though your children may ask your advice, it is often better if you ask what they think. If you have done the best job you know how in raising your son or daughter, then they already have a wealth of experience with which to draw from. What I mean is, more than likely they have the answer inside of them, and all they need is your reassurance that they can figure out this problem for themselves. That kind of reassurance builds self-confidence. We all need self-confidence, right?

Study Guide Questions

1. How old is your son?

2. What is your idea of giving advice to your son or daughter?

3. How do you respond if your advice is not accepted?

4. What kind of advice were you given as a young adult?

5. What advice would you like your son to follow?

Chapter Five
Peter Pan

When I was little, I was fascinated with the Peter Pan story and wondered what I could do to fly. Being able to do whatever he wanted, Peter Pan seemed to have the perfect life. Later my kids and I saw the movie *Hook,* a sequel to the original Peter Pan story, and I had a better understanding of the movie's plot. What I took away from the story was that children needed their mother or else they end up in a Neverland (of their own) and they don't grow into well-rounded adults. Peter Pan was a lonely man/boy.

You've met the Peter Pans of the world. They are the men who can't commit to relationships, are easily drawn to the next challenge; never establishing roots anywhere with the possible exception of their parents' home. And by the way, their parents don't see them very often. Sometimes Peter Pan is a man who has fathered several children by different women and is never around to watch them grow up or to financially support them. He can't commit to the woman of his dreams and he drifts through life.

A Peter Pan personality is also developed when he grows up in a home with parents, who are too busy to spend time with him, or who are physically present, but not emotionally present. While there are many reasons a parent may not be engaged with their child, the boy still suffers.

What causes a boy not to want to grow up? Did he have a wonderful childhood that ended when his parents divorced or died, and he wasn't able to move past that period of his life? Was he not allowed to be a child because he had so many responsibilities that his time for childhood slipped away? Did his parents take such good care of him that they didn't allow him to make decisions for himself or allow him to stretch his wings and grow into a man? There are probably a number of scenarios that keep a young boy from maturing into an adult man. Some may miss their mothers. Mothers are the rudders, the bearer of moral values, the heart and conscience of the family. As such, she validates feelings and allows her sons to establish their own internal moral barometers. That is not to say that men don't contain these type of internal registers, it is just that in our society men are not conditioned to stay in touch with their feelings, so they usually do not value that part of their personality unless they had someone at home, mom or a mom type, who continued to keep them in touch with their sensitive side.

If you remember, Peter Pan didn't have a mom, so one could say that he was never conditioned to being sensitive and having good morals. He was a boy who enjoyed doing what he wanted and seeing the other boys fight and steal. The Lost Boys broke societal rules all the time and nobody cared. That was part of Peter Pan's problem. In everyday life, the Peter Pans of the world may or may not break societal rules, however, they may continue to struggle with the confines of relationship commitments, and shy away from heartfelt friendships.

How do you help your son if he is a Peter Pan type? Reestablish a relationship with him. Maybe you had to give him up for adoption because you were too young to raise him (and he doesn't know you). Maybe you lost custody because of issues that were going on in your life, and years have passed, but now you want to get to know that son. It may take a while, but if you know how to get in touch with him, make an attempt to do so. Initial contact may be rocky and he may resent you trying to establish contact, but establishing a relationship with your son or daughter is the essence of parenthood. Better late than never!

---

[6] 1991 American fantasy film directed by Steven Spielberg

Study Guide Questions

1. Do you know someone who has trouble committing to relationships? If yes, please explain.

2. What kind of childhood would contribute to a person with a Peter Pan personality?

3. List the steps you would take if you wanted to reestablish contact with your son?

Chapter Six
Male Role Models

When I was a teenager, my parents divorced. While it was hard on all of us my brother really suffered the most. He was the youngest, but I don't believe that's why he suffered; he missed the male companionship that my dad offered. Mind you, the two of them, my dad and brother, did not do 'male bonding things' together. They didn't work out together or fish or play tennis or bike, but having another person that embodies who you are, is often enough – at least temporarily. Once the divorce was final and my dad had moved out of the house, my brother got into all types of trouble where he had to be rescued either by my father or my uncle. Even if his consequence was a spanking, it was a form of attention from his role model, his dad. While I was young at the time, I could see that my brother was not as concerned about the consequence he would receive as much as receiving the attention from my dad, even if it was negative reinforcement. He wanted our dad's attention! I resented the fact that while my dad wasn't around often, he would come around to dole out punishment to my brother. He could have used my first book about parenting teens!

My brother lived in a painful, private world, and during the time that I was away at college, I didn't see his melt-downs as often as my mother and sister did. In retrospect, I just wish my dad had spent more quality time with my brother. Of course, my dad was also a loner during his formative years, so he could only model what he knew. Right? As an adult, I now realize that he could only give what he received. However, I resented my father for a long time as a result of his perceived lack of relationship with my brother. I could not understand how he could talk so easily to me, yet not reach out to my brother. Years later, after raising sons and teaching high school boys, I have learned that there are unwritten rules of engagement when it comes to interacting with boys. According to Dan Kindlon and Michael Thompson, authors of *Raising Cain*, 'our culture's dominant masculine stereotypes shortchange boys and lead them toward emotional isolation'.

Male role models are necessary because men and boys process information in similar ways. Boys watch everything their dads do. For example, if their relationship is close, boys watch their fathers shave or put on their tie, cologne, tie their shoes, you name it. Boys want to do it the exact same way. Women can't offer that kind of modeling for their sons. Another example is when my husband talks to my son. There is a man-speak language going on. My husband and I can say the same words, but coming from my husband, there seems to be a different level of respect (that he receives) than when I talk to my son.

Jennie from Oak Park was talking to her son's teacher during a parent-teacher conference, and her son Johnny was having a horrible school year. His grades were terrible. When she asked him what was going on, he told her to leave him alone and turned away from Jennie. When Johnny's male teacher asked him what the problem was, he answered the teacher. I have had many conversations with female parents and their sons. On many occasions, the son is derisive and disrespectful, and the mom fusses with him – 'Don't talk to me like that'. Yet, when a father figure, male relative, mentor or coach says the same thing to that boy, the boy listens. Why is he more inclined to listen to the male voice and not yours? Good question..

The age of your son, will determine what tools you will need to best communicate with him. If he is a young child, then you and your son are pals and he is more inclined to listen when you give him instructions. He wants to be around you 24/7 and cries if you leave his side. However, as I mentioned in Chapter 2 on the Oedipus complex, once he reaches seven or eight years of age, he starts to distance himself from you and identify more with boys his age and the male figures in his life. You may find at this age that he half listens to you and you often find yourself repeating instructions. If you aren't careful, you will find yourself yelling at him for something he has not done. Yet, his father or another man won't necessarily have the same problem. I would encourage you to have a conversation about it.

Moms who continue to stay in tune with their sons, stay consistent in their parenting, provide stability, love, fun and discipline tend to continue to have rewarding relationships with their sons well into their son's teenage years. It's quite okay to listen to his music or play video games with him. He has to feel safe around you and know that you won't betray him. I had a parent tell me that their son never talked. I didn't find that to be true at all because as my student, the young man told me all kinds of things. One of the things I learned from my students was how much they had to say. They didn't mind sharing their innermost secrets because I didn't judge them for their thoughts and feelings. If I thought they were headed into dangerous territory, I told them so and also contacted the school counselor or their parent if I needed to.

However, I will never be a man, so I really can't be an effective male role model. If you are a single mother, it is extremely important for you to help your son maintain ties with his father, older brother, uncle or grandfather. With all of the emotional ups and downs that your son is facing (daily), he needs someone to talk to that he can trust (and is trustworthy); someone that will have your son's best interests at heart. Getting issues and concerns out, helps eliminate the anger and frustration that your son may have. Pent up anger and frustration causes boys (girls too) to make poor decisions that can change their lives forever. There are lots of angry men and women in prison or in their graves. Let's try to reduce that statistic, one boy at a time.

---

[7] *Raising Cain* – published by Ballantine Books

Study Guide Questions

1. Is your son's father involved in his life?

2. Does he live with your son, if not please explain?

3. What kind of relationship does/did your husband have with his father?

4. Who are the role models in your son's life?

5. Write what you think it takes to become an effective role model to your son.

Chapter Seven

The More We Push

When I was growing up, my mom constantly prodded, cajoled and pushed me to be a better person than I was. She said, "Be smarter, neater, more thoughtful, etc., etc., etc.". While I wasn't a mental giant by any means, as she continued to push, I responded. Of course, I had my own ideas of what I wanted to do, but I also wanted to please my mother, so I tried my best to be the daughter I thought she wanted me to be. Unfortunately for her, I was opinionated and strong-willed; I didn't willingly go along with the plans my parents had for me. I had my own mind! Maybe if I wasn't so strong-willed, she wouldn't have had to push so hard. My point is that I tried to respond as an obedient child, but more often than not, I was a recalcitrant, questioning young person. If I was told not to do something, I had to try it anyway because I needed to check it out for myself. My sister was quite obedient and didn't bend the rules much. She was a good girl and was really afraid of doing anything that would anger my mom or dad.

My brother on the other hand, was a lot like me and we both stayed in trouble. The more my parents pushed, the more we were determined to do things our way. I must admit that I responded better to my parents if ideas were suggested to me (instead of told to me) and I had a choice. Who am I fooling? Suggesting things was for permissive parents and my parents were crazy and strict, so I was often at odds with them. This is true for many strong-willed children, but especially for strong-willed sons.

My daughter had her own ideas of how she wanted to proceed, but she wasn't headstrong and argumentative. She was quite talkative. She talked so much that I would worry when she stopped talking. My son talked less, but we had to watch him because he was much more active than our daughter and as he got older, his internal sensibilities made him a difficult force to reckon with. He had a strong will and wasn't concerned if what he felt was not in line with his father or me. He operated with his own internal sense of order and process. By that I mean that it didn't matter if his father or I disagreed with what he wanted to do. If it made sense to him, it was worth pursuing. He was the kid that reminded us that he was to get a spanking because he disobeyed our rules. Who does that? He was also the kid that would argue a subject into the next day. Ridiculous, but that's how he is engineered. However as a late teen, when he felt safe, he would follow me around the house talking incessantly about one subject or another.

What do I mean by 'feeling safe'? If a child opens

up to you and you are open to him or her, non-judgmental and actively listening, they will tell you lots about them; that is what I mean by feeling safe.

I noticed two important points when parenting my son. Be patient; stop yelling or screaming at him and seek to have a conversation with your son. Some boys may respond to pushing, prodding and yelling, but it comes with a price. Like our husbands, they eventually stop listening to you and tune you out. If you aren't careful, you may miss the cues. While strong-willed people are usually more vocal about what they like and don't like, quiet types won't talk at all. As a matter of fact, your son may do whatever is necessary to avoid interacting with you. He may look directly at you like he is listening, but his mind is a thousand miles away. When our son didn't want to interact with us, he would tell us he wasn't hungry and would wait until we were in another part of the house to eat, even if it was late at night. He would stay in his room to avoid interacting with us. This was just to avoid conversations or (in his mind) a confrontation about an issue or topic he wasn't ready to discuss.

I don't know about you, but I didn't like this part of parenting at all! It's hard when our sons put up barriers to communicating with us. Once I have identified a problem (in this case – my beloved son), I prefer to talk about it and figure out how we can solve the problem. That's how mothers approach problems. Children don't always respond to that approach, especially boys. They put up walls that are almost impossible to move beyond and have meaningful conversation. Contrary to popular belief, boys are just as sensitive as girls, and may want to avoid conflict as much as possible, while they are hurting inside. If you have a son who is using drugs, running with the wrong crowd, has dropped out of school or is being bullied, these topics require honest discussion, as well as ways to help your son work through these issues.

So how do you marry tough love with wise parenting? The tough love part of this relationship story is realizing that you cannot allow your son's inappropriate behavior to continue, thinking that it will miraculously go away. The issue(s) have to be addressed. The wise parenting part of it is picking the best time to talk and piggybacking on 'good times' where everyone is relaxed and open to discussion. This is a good time to check your ego at the door, and be open to what you may hear during your dialogue with your son. Be humble and honest.

I think sometimes, parents feel that because of our position as parents, we are above reproach. "You're my son and I will not allow you to talk to me like that!" That kind of attitude can be an accelerant to an already fiery situation. In our household, our children were able to say what was on their minds as long as they were respectful and didn't use profanity. That worked well in most situations; however, depending upon what kind of situation your son may find himself involved in, his conversation may not be forthcoming at all. What do you do in that situation? Cajoling and pushing are the last things you want to do. Be intentional and set up a time where you, your son, and his father, grandfather or uncle can talk together. By the way, ignore ringing cell phones or house phones until you are done talking. Being intentional means you are completely present and will not allow normal distractions to deter good conversation.

I find that situations where your son is ashamed or disillusioned, coming to a meaningful solution may take more time and several separate conversations. Be prepared and give yourself and your son the time necessary to work through the situation satisfactorily. I know one family where the son loves ice cream. When the mom wanted to have meaningful conversation, she would take her son for ice cream and they would sit and talk. Her son's guard was down and it was easier to start talking. I find starting with any subject excluding the one you want to talk about allows you to ease into the conversation.

At this point, hopefully you are aware of the simple pleasures that your son loves, and have enjoyed some of those pleasures with him. It's hard to mitigate a situation if you have not established a relationship with your son. Wise parenting is a trial and error process. It requires your time and effort. You might think, 'I give him money and he has the latest gym shoes and video games, what more could he want?' In this day of instant convenience and ever changing technology, good old-fashioned relationships cannot be purchased. They are earned.

Shame has no place here either. How many times

have you seen your son cry and said, 'Oh stop whining', or 'You're crying like a girl', or any of those phrases that negate your son's feelings? Boys do have feelings, and a wise parent allows those feelings to be part of their relationship without making the son feel that he has to be a non-feeling macho type. Crying is not just for girls. By the way, not all girls show their emotions by crying either. (Read my next book for girl discovery.) Sometimes boys experience rage as a vehicle to respond to situations where they just can't cope. This is not a 'Boys will be boys' moment, or 'He responds just like his father'. Stop the nonsense! Punching a hole in the wall or breaking a window with your fist is a fit of out of control rage. Those kinds of acting out moments need to be discussed and boys need to be given tools to help better manage moments that cause rage, so that they do not become prison or mortuary statistics.

Study Guide Questions

1. What kinds of activities do you and your son enjoy together?

2. How do you respond to your son when he is fearful?

3. What kind of parenting style do you have?

4. Are you pleased with your son's current success? If you answered no, what would you like to see him do differently? Please explain.

Chapter Eight
Discipline

If your idea of discipline is to say, "Don't do that, Danny", and you don't follow up with a stronger message when Danny continues to disobey your rules, then understand that talking as a form of discipline may not work for Danny especially if he is a strong-willed child. Spanking may not work either.

The Webster's dictionary defines discipline as a training that corrects, molds, or perfects the mental faculties or moral character; control gained by enforcing obedience or order.[8] There are two main schools of thought when it comes to the most effective form of discipline. Some parents believe that discipline should be harsh and swift; others believe that you have to allow the child to find himself, and he will naturally do the right thing. It does not matter which school of thought you subscribe to if your son continues to misbehave. Misbehavior is an old-fashioned term used when the child breaks the rules whether occasionally or often. What do you do when you have a child that continues to break the rules and openly defies you? What form of discipline do you institute then?

The real issue is what is your belief system and how were you raised? I conducted a recent survey of parents to get their thoughts on spanking. Out of 50 parents, fifty percent believed corporal punishment, (another name for spanking) should be used only if other means of discipline had not worked and the child was under the age of ten. Spanking is considered barbaric by many parents and in our society now, you can get arrested if you spank your child in public because it is seen as a form of abuse. Those that opposed spanking believed that it encouraged violence in our children.

What is your idea of a spanking? Is it tapping your child's behind with your hand or using a 'switch'? My grandmother used a switch occasionally and if a switch was needed, I had to go to the tree in the backyard and bring her a young branch, which she would use to administer her form of justice. I don't think she had to use a switch on me but once. It was quite a behavior adjuster!

Just 30-40 years ago, not only did your parents spank you, but neighbors and teachers were allowed to spank you if you disobeyed. Any adult that had to reprimand you could do so without your parents getting mad at them. If the adult or teacher had to reprimand you, they usually called your house and told your parents that they had to reprimand you, and then you also got punished for being reprimanded by another adult.

Administering time-out was also a form of discipline that parents found useful. However, the maximum age for effective use of time-out was considered six. So what happens when your son is ten and tells you to 'Go to hell'? What do you do?

Discipline is such a hot issue that I did some faith-based research. In one of the Old Testament passages, it says, "A fool despises his father's instruction, but he who receives correction is prudent."[9] Another passage refers to God's wrath when doing things which are not fitting, one of which was to be disobedient to parents. Some Muslims believe that caning their children is the only form of discipline that brings results.

A Vietnamese friend of mine once told me that in her culture, parents often caned their children long into their adult years. By the way, caning[11] is a form of punishment consisting of a number of hits to a part of the body made with a single cane, usually made of rattan. The Talmud talks about discipline being vital to raising a healthy child, but physical means of discipline should never occur. Now maybe the rod that King Solomon spoke about was a metaphor for doling out tough love. The United Methodist Church believes that Jesus Christ would not condone any action that would cause harm to children physically or emotionally.[1] Buddhists believe that emotional or physical pain, create fear and trauma.[13] Different cultures handle the discipline of children in different ways. What is most important to remember is that some form of loving discipline should take place in order to raise a healthy son or daughter.

When my son was younger, I used to tell him that God held me accountable for how I raised him; his success or failure was directly related to me and his father. One of the stories that left a significant impression upon me was the story of Eli and his sons. Eli was an influential high priest and judge in Israel in Old Testament times. He had two sons, who acted as the priest's servants, but they did not know God. Therefore, when they worked in the temple, they were disrespectful and often took what they wanted from the sacrifices that people offered to God. The Bible says the sons dishonored God by conducting their priestly duties with irreverence.[14] They were also sexually disrespectful to the women assembled at the door of the tabernacle. Eli talked to his sons, but his protests were weak and the sons disregarded Eli's words. God considered Eli's rebuke of his sons weak and ineffective, felt Eli favored his sons over God himself, and held Eli accountable for his sons' lack of discipline and respect. As a result, God destroyed Eli, and his two sons. I wasn't sure if Eli was ultimately punished because he didn't discipline his sons, or because he spoiled his sons until they were completely rotten. In other words, Eli needed better parenting skills! I wish Eli had read my first parenting book!

As I said earlier, that passage of scripture made a tremendous impact on me, and I have been determined to teach my children to be respectful, honorable, well-adjusted and healthy people. While I will not tell you one form of discipline is better than the other, I do believe you should establish guidelines in your home and hold your son and daughter accountable to uphold those rules and to be honorable people. Headlines in many newspapers today, point to out of control people, but especially violent and out of control teens. Your teen's years are traumatic enough with raging hormones and immaturity, but without love, guidelines, boundaries, faith, respect and discipline, your son's life is doomed before he reaches the age of eighteen.

Whether you believe in a higher power or no power at all, it is important to apply love and discipline to your arsenal of parenting techniques in order to shape your son into the man that you will be proud to call your son.

[8] http://www.merriam-webster.com/dictionary/discipline
[9] Proverbs 15:5, The Nelson Study Bible - NKJV
[10] Romans 1:30, The Nelson Study Bible - NKJV
[11] Wikipedia - http://en.wikipedia.org/wiki/Caning
[12] http://www.stophitting.com/index.php?page=unitedmethodist
[13] http://www.stophitting.com/index.php?page=buddhistonpunish
[14] 1 Samuel 2:17, The Nelson Study Bible - NKJV

Study Guide Questions

1. Do you believe in discipline for your son? If yes, explain what discipline means in your household.

2. Discuss how you were raised? How was discipline handled when you were a child?

3. How tolerant are you of your child's disobedience?

Chapter Nine
Just Let Go. *How?*

There may come a time in your relationship with your son when you will have to part ways, stop trying to control his activities/behavior or at the very least cease worrying that he won't succeed without your 24-hour a day assistance. I am not trying to be sarcastic, but you will know the time once it rears its ugly head.

If you are a spiritual person, then relinquishing control is not something that is new to you. Letting go is a concept where you stop fighting and begin to accept the person for who or what they are. It is usually a process that takes place when you leave a person who you love, but can't seem to work things out with; usually a husband or boyfriend. Many religions are familiar with the concept of letting go and letting a Higher Power take over. If you are used to exerting control over your child and telling him what to do, this process will feel unfamiliar and uncomfortable to you. However, if your son is over the age of fifteen, will not listen to reasonable suggestions or worse yet, continues to ignore or disrespect you, then letting him go will be the best option that you can offer your son.

In addition to the spiritual aspect of letting go, consider no longer paying his car note, rent, cell phone bill, washing his laundry or the myriad of activities that you are performing to 'help' your son succeed. In order to grow into successful men, our sons really like being independent and being autonomous from us parents. There is really no way to allow them to develop that independence if we continue pulling out the life boats. I don't know about you, but if my son was too quiet I wanted to know what was wrong. Obviously, if your son has multiple days of silence, you will want to talk with him and find out if there is anything wrong. If there are no unusual problems then just let him go and leave him to figure out a solution to his problem! I believe humans are the only species on the planet that hover indefinitely over their young. How in the world do we expect them to grow up, if we are constantly tying them to our apron strings?

What exactly is letting go? Sometimes, if you are divorced, it means letting your son live with his dad, an act that you consider unthinkable because your ex-husband can hardly take care of himself. In the movie, Life as a House[15], the son lived with his mom and stepdad. As a high school aged teen, he was moody, skipping classes, using drugs, badly influencing his younger brother and both ignoring his parents' wishes and arguing with them on most details. While his mother was vehemently opposed to her ex-husband, Kevin

Kline's lifestyle (she felt her ex-husband was irresponsible); she agreed that her son (played by Hayden Christensen) should spend the summer living with his father. She lets her son go, and amazing things started to happen. You will have to see the movie to find out the details and the extraordinary ending. My point is that we don't have to continue to beat our heads against the wall trying to understand and relate to our sons. This time is an opportunity for our sons to test the waters and exert their adolescent influence upon their life. Your son is not intentionally trying to defy your every command; he is just trying to grow up.

Surprisingly, you are the closest person to him. I know it doesn't feel that way right now because he hasn't said a civil word to you in days. Just give him room to grow and mature a bit. Try not to question his every move and thought. Remember he has to distance himself from you as his mother and find himself as a man, like his father. While you are giving him the space to grow, also continue to make time for things you two like to do together. During our time together, we listen to my son's music or go to movies that we both enjoy. It opens the space for talk time, and it is non-confrontational and comforting.

Just because he is growing up, does not mean he has lost the need for the nurturing closeness of his mother.

---

[15] *Life as a House* is a 2001 American drama film produced and directed by Irwin Winkler

Study Guide Questions

1. What does 'Letting Go' mean to you?

2. Explain how you would let go of your son.

3. What kind of relationship do you currently share with your son? Is there room for improvement? If so, please explain.

Chapter Ten
She's Not Good Enough for You

What is it that mothers see in other women that make those women not good enough for their sons? What characteristics do we as mothers expect to see in our sons' girlfriends, significant others or wives? Are we expecting the women to act like us, kowtow to us, dress and look perfect; a perfection that we ourselves don't have? Or could it be that we have nurtured these boys all of their lives and we want them to become involved with or marry women like us? We've trained our boys to know what a good girl is, because those are the girls that they bring home for us to meet. The other girls or women are ones that they may hang out with, sleep with, but in the final analysis, don't marry.

But, what about the girls that are in our opinion, 'good girls'? Good girls dress appropriately and are well educated. Maybe they are outspoken, or simply have a rapport with your son, that indicates the son is not listening to you as much as he used to and prefers to "be with" her. We often consider those women not good enough either. Why do we consider those women not good enough? Is it because we won't be able to control them if they marry our sons? Or could those women be more like us than we care to admit? In any event, we push away our sons when we exhibit those perfectionist tendencies that urge us to tell our sons, "She's not good enough for you".

I had a friend who was a 'good girl'. She had good home training, was well-educated, came from a good family and yet when she met her boyfriend's (later her husband) parents for the first time, his mother was very standoffish and unfriendly. As I remember, the woman was a member of a different church denomination and was probably more outspoken than the other girls he brought home. He fell head over heels for the young woman and married her. My point is that our role as mothers is to help raise and nurture our sons to the best of our ability, but not smother them. You notice I said help raise. That means you can't do it alone. Our boys also need a father figure in their lives, if not the father himself. We covered that in Chapter 6.

How important is your son's relationship to you? Pretty important, right? Are you two close and have a good relationship, or is your relationship fractured and heart-breaking? What are the spiritual expectations of us as mothers? God holds us accountable for raising our boys according to his teachings. Below are some spiritual principles that I relied on when raising my sons was beyond my level of experience.

- Take a couple of deep breaths before reacting

- Do not provoke your children to anger; but bring them up in the discipline and instruction of the Lord.

- I am the adult and I choose how I will respond to my child.

- Divine order is the order of the day.

- Help me to be the best mom that I can be.

Study Guide Questions

1. Write down the kind of relationship that you currently have with your son(s)?

2. What kind of relationship would you like to have with your son(s)?

3. What type of girl is an acceptable girl for your son to meet and date?

4. If you have used the phrase 'she's not good enough for you,' what did you mean?

Chapter Eleven
Respect and Honor

Please and thank you go a long way, but that is not what this chapter is about. Let's talk about talking to and treating our sons (and daughters) the way we want to be treated---with honor and respect. I grew up in a household where we were taught to respect each other. I didn't have to say "yes ma'am" and "no sir," but I couldn't say 'Huh' or 'What' when my parents called me. We were taught to make eye contact with our parents. 'Look at me when I'm talking to you' was not a phrase I wanted to hear often. We also had to listen to any adults anywhere if they had something to say to us. There was no such thing as disrespecting an adult. Rolling your eyes was not something you did if you wanted to continue to see out of those eyes, so respect was an important part of my upbringing.

In my childhood, my parents knew everybody, so I never knew who reported back to them if they saw me in a place that I shouldn't have been. There was always some adult watching out for me. At least I thought so. Occasionally, when we did something dumb, our dad called us numbskulls or told us how stupid something was, but he and my mother never cursed us out; we were never told that we wouldn't amount to anything, or some of the really awful language that I hear parents say to their children today.

As a result of how my parents treated me, I treated my children with respect. The one time that I cursed at my kids, I remember being really frustrated with them. Something had happened that didn't make sense and I was tired. During the night God reminded me that he never cursed at me and I had done some really dumb things. So why was I cursing at my children that I loved dearly? I got the message loud and clear! I never cursed at them again.

That doesn't mean that you won't get mad at them; of course that will happen. However, you are the adult in this relationship, and if you have an explosive temper, you have to learn appropriate ways to control it. How do you expect your son to respect and honor other people when his own parent—YOU, can't control yourself? My son was familiar with the time-out concept, so it was amusing to him when I used it to control myself. If I thought I was losing my cool, I would tell my children it was time-out time for mom. I usually didn't need more than ten minutes. But it gave me time to collect my thoughts, think about what happened, usually say a quick prayer for Divine Order, and then I was ready to deal with my son or daughter.

If you are the type of person who uses profanity, think about how completely terrible it sounds coming out of the mouth of a three-year-old? Your three year old son should not know how to say the F-word.

And, while I said this chapter wasn't about please and thank you, those are two phrases that should be well established in your household. You may be thinking why do I have to say please and thank you to members of my family? They know I mean please and thank you, right? However, you expect people outside of your family to be polite and well-mannered, don't you? This is not an intuitive skill that you can turn on and off. It's learned behavior, and if you want a polite, well-mannered son, you have to teach and model the behavior that you want to see him exhibit. It's funny; you may not notice how out of order your son's behavior is until you meet one of his friends who has been taught to be respectful, polite, even holding the doors open for other people. Your son cannot model that behavior if you haven't taught him that behavior. Mothers, you may think that as a single parent, you don't have a suitable role model for your son to mimic. Well, have him practice holding the doors open for you, his sister, his grandmother or aunt. Have him help the lady across the street carry her groceries into the house or shovel the snow for the elderly couple down the street (without charging them money). There are lots of teachable moments that you can use to help your son learn how to be respectable.

Now let's address honor. Dictionary.com[16] defines honor as honesty, fairness, or integrity in one's beliefs and actions. A man of honor doesn't decide to become a man of honor at the age of 21 or 25. He learned different lessons along the way that helped him become a man of honor. Your son cannot operate with honor and integrity if you don't discipline him when he comes home with something that doesn't belong to him.

I remember my brother had a toy that he started playing with that my mom and dad had not purchased and that he had not received as a gift from relatives or friends. After grilling him about it, they found out that he had 'borrowed' the toy from the local store without paying for it. Of course he was punished and made to return the 'borrowed' item immediately. Many times, people legitimately lose things and your son may have actually found someone's wallet. However if that happens, do you require that he contact the person and return it or do you say "Finders Keepers, Losers Weepers" or however that phrase goes? Remember you are using teachable moments to help him grow up honorably.

My own son took a piece of candy from a local store and I noticed it when we got into the car. I marched him right back into the store and made him apologize for taking the candy. Even as a young boy, he experienced embarrassment. I didn't care, because it taught him to be accountable. I told him that God held me accountable for how he was raised, and I definitely wanted his young life to be pleasing to God. Accountability is not a trait that is well respected or that is often taught in our society anymore. And yet, when you read about someone who has stolen millions from others, or who has committed a crime, if you look into the person's past, you may find that he was not often held accountable for his actions while he was growing into manhood. How do you expect to be an honorable person when you have been trained to be a social misfit?

Webster's Dictionary defines integrity as moral soundness; honesty; freedom from corrupting influence or motive. Accountability is the willingness to be responsible for one's own actions. These are traits that are considered passé and not valued much in our society today. We must include them in our arsenal of parenting tools to ensure that our sons and daughters become well-rounded and respectable adults.

Would you allow me to also add a note about dress code? I realize that we live in a very relaxed society these days and it's a 'Come as you please' environment. While I agree with that to a point, there are many times when appropriate dress code does not mean wearing a pair of jeans and a t-shirt. I was taught that first impressions are lasting impressions. Even if all of the social locations that you and your son frequent have relaxed dress codes, your son needs to understand when he needs to be appropriately dressed. It may be okay to dress down for school or work, however, people still judge you by your appearance. Unfortunately, the guy sitting across the desk from your son in an interview does not know how smart your son is if all he can see is his pants are hanging lower than his boxers, or his hair and face are unkempt, or he has a number of tattoos or body piercings, or he is wearing sunglasses and a baseball cap. Don't get me wrong, I grew up in the sixties and am an original flower child, so I believe in self-expression. However, when I was ready to interview for a job or scholarship, I knew that I had to assimilate into the mainstream culture that would employ me. Nobody cares that your son wants to express himself, unless he is self-employed and his line of work is unique and self-sustaining.

I also believe that what goes around comes around. So if you buy the TV or iPod from someone off the street, don't be surprised if at some point, your house is burglarized and your TV or iPod are stolen. It is just the spiritual law of Karma working itself out. I'm digressing here, but the point that I want you to take away from this chapter is that as his parent, you want your son to grow into a wonderful, successful person who is respectable, respectful and honorable. Not only do you want him to treat his immediate family well, you also want him to treat the ordinary person on the street well. Do your part to make that happen.

---

[17] http://www.webster-dictionary.org/definition/integrity
[18] http://www.merriam-webster.com/dictionary/accountability

Study Guide Questions

1. What does it mean to be respectable and honorable in your family?

2. How do you handle yourself when other adults correct your son's behavior?

3. Do you believe that it takes a village to raise a child? Explain your answer with examples.

4. Do you believe respect and honor should be demonstrated by parents? Please explain

Epilogue

As I was completing my first book, I started thinking about the relationship that I had with my two sons, as well as the relationship that I had established with other young men that I had met either through my children or had taught throughout the years. I had some amazing discoveries and Aha moments, as well as many sleepless nights. One of my discoveries was that it didn't really matter if the son belonged to me or someone else. When he had a problem, I made myself available to help him work it out.

As human beings, I believe that it is our role to help each other out. I also learned that it was okay not to have all of the answers to questions that my young men asked. I promised that I would attempt to find the answer, and I often did. In standing up for and to my students, I learned to be a better parent, and when I became a better parent, I became a better educator.

Parenting is not for the faint-hearted. You will have life-changing experiences. Parenting is a life-time commitment and it can be all-consuming. However it is one of the most rewarding relationships I have ever had. Love and enjoy your son but don't place him on a pedestal. He is human and needs your love, support, and discipline, just like your daughter. Make him proud to be your son, and be proud to be his mom.

I welcome your thoughts and comments. Email me at: cgwwbooks@yahoo.com.

I would love to discuss your thoughts and ideas at my blogsite: http://authorclynnwilliams.wordpress.com/

Best wishes to you and your family

C. Lynn Williams
aka MsParentguru

Additional Resources

At the end of my presentations or workshops, participants often ask where they can go for more information about parenting, especially when they need assistance with deeper issues like mental illness, divorce, violent behaviors or adoption. I have included a list of resources which may be helpful to parents, psychologists, physicians or educators.

Resources Dealing with Parenting Boys

Dobson, J. *Bringing Up Boys*. Tyndale House Publishers, 2005. Dr. James Dobson gives advice and encouragement on raising boys using a foundation of biblical principles.

Kindlon, D., Thompson, M., Barker, T. *Raising Cain*. Ballantine Books, 2000. An expert in child development from Harvard and a preeminent child psychologist offer groundbreaking guidance for parents and educators of boys in crisis. Their book explains the physical and emotional well-being of teenage boys and the unique risks and dangers that they face.

Franklin, A. (Ph.D.). *From Brotherhood to Manhood: How Black Men Rescue Their Relationships and Dreams from the Invisibility Syndrome.* **Wiley, 2002.** Gives a psychologist's point of view and perspective for parents who have to teach their young African-American off-spring core values and offers advice to inspire men from any background.

[Website]. Depression in Young and Teenage Boys. http://www.medicinenet.com/script/main/art.as p?articlekey=23376

[Website]. Mental Illness in Children. http://www.medicinenet.com/mental_illness_in_ children/article.htm

[Website]. Local Resources for Mental Illness in Children. http://www.medicinenet.com/mental_illness_ in_ children/city.htm

[Website]. Clinical and Child Psychology. The Therapist Directory. http://www.psychology.com/ therapist/

12966468R00053

Made in the USA
Charleston, SC
08 June 2012